ent

Encore Folio
for CLARINET
WITH PIANO ACCOMPANIMENT

RUBANK®

HAL•LEONARD® CORPORATION
7777 W. BLUEMOUND RD. P.O. BOX 13819 MILWAUKEE, WI 53213

Nocturne

from
Midsummer Night's Dream

Piano acc.

FELIX MENDELSSOHN
German 1809-1847
Arr. by Henry W. Davis

Copyright MCMXXXVII by Rubank Inc., Chicago, Ill.
International Copyright Secured

Spirit Dance

from the Opera
ORPHEUS

Piano acc.

CHRISTOPHER WILLIBALD von GLUCK
German 1714-1787
Arr. by Henry W. Davis

Copyright MCMXXXVII by Rubank Inc., Chicago, Ill.
International Copyright Secured

Andante
from
Pathetic Symphony

Piano acc.

P. TSCHAIKOWSKY Op. 74
Russian 1840-1893
Arr. by Henry W. Davis

Copyright MCMXXXVII by Rubank Inc.,Chicago,Ill.
International Copyright Secured

304-2

Intermezzo

from
Cavalleria Rusticana

Piano acc.

P. MASCAGNI
Italian Dec. 7, 1863-
Arr. by Henry W. Davis

Unfinished Symphony
Themes from First Movement

Piano acc.

FRANZ SCHUBERT
Austria 1797-1828
Arr by Henry W Davis

Copyright MCMXXXVII by Rubannk Inc.,Chicago,Ill.
International Copyright Secured

302-3

302-3

13
Barcarolle
from
Tales of Hoffmann

Piano acc.

J. OFFENBACH
German-1819-1880
Arr. by Henry W. Davis

Copyright MCMXXXVII by Rubank Inc.,Chicago,Ill.
International Copyright Secured

307-3

307-3

Largo
from
New World Symphony

Piano acc.

ANTON DVOŘÁK
Bohemia = 1841-1904
Arr. by Henry W. Davis

Copyright MCMXXXVII by Rubank Inc., Chicago, III.
International Copyright Secured

314-3

Sleeping Beauty

Waltz Theme from the Ballet

Piano

P. TSCHAIKOWSKY
Russian 1840-1893
Arr. by Henry W. Davis

Copyright MCMXXXVII by Rubank Inc., Chicago, Ill.
International Copyright Secured

322-4

Chansonette

Piano

A. M. BARRET
Arr. by A.W. Pazemis

888-3

Song of the Dawn

(Chanson d'Aurore)

from

Suite Miniature for Clarinet

Piano

A. GRETCHANINOFF, Op. 145, No. 1
EDITED by H. Voxman

903-2

Fanfare of the Poppies

(Fanfare de Coquelicots)

from

Suite Miniature for Clarinet

Piano

A. GRETCHANINOFF, Op.145, No.5
Edited by H. Voxman

905-2

Encore Folio

for C L A R I N E T

WITH PIANO ACCOMPANIMENT

RUBANK®

HAL•LEONARD®
CORPORATION

7777 W. BLUEMOUND RD. P.O. BOX 13819 MILWAUKEE, WI 53213

Nocturne
from
Midsummer Night's Dream

Mendelssohn at the age of 12 began to compose. His genius made it possible to write many outstanding works.

The Nocturne is the incidental music played between the 3rd and 4th Acts of Mendelssohn's settings to Shakespeare's "A Midsummer Night's Dream."

FELIX MENDELSSOHN
German 1809-1847
Arr. by Henry W. Davis

Solo Bb Clarinet

Copyright MCMXXXVII by Rubank Inc.,Chicago,Ill.
International Copyright Secured

Spirit ³Dance
from the Opera
ORPHEUS

Gluck was a disciple of the Italian school of opera which dominated the musical world of the eighteenth century, but became disgusted with its triviality, and in Paris instituted a reform movement that not only anticipated Wagner, but prepared the way for that master. The opera Orpheus was written at the time he began composing in his later style.

Solo B♭ Clarinet

CHRISTOPHER WILLIBALD von GLUCK
German 1714-1787
Arr. by Henry W. Davis

4
Andante
from
Pathetic Symphony

A great modern composer, whose compositions stir the hearts of music lovers throughout the world. This Andante Theme portrays that deep gloom and melancholy feeling of a once oppressed people. Tschaikowsky called this Sixth Symphony "The Pathetic" after hearing its first performance.

B♭ Clarinet

P. TSCHAIKOWSKY Op.74
Russian 1840-1893
Arr. by Henry W Davis

303-1

Intermezzo
from
Cavalleria Rusticana

This is a one act opera in two scenes depicting a tragedy in the lives of simple peasants in a Sicilian village. During the first scene, the villagers are entering a church for Easter services. The curtain descends and this beautiful melody is played between the scenes. At its close the curtain rises to reveal the villagers leaving the church.

Bb Clarinet

P. MASCAGNI
Italian Dec. 7, 1863 -
Arr. by Henry W. Davis

Copyright MCMXXXVII by Rubank Inc., Chicago, Ill.
International Copyright Secured

Unfinished Symphony
Themes from First Movement

Schubert was born near Vienna. He began composing at High School Age. Although most of his compositions were not appreciated during his short life-time, today he ranks among the immortals.

The Unfinished Symphony begun in 1822, was never finished and is one of the mysteries of music history.

B♭ Clarinet

FRANZ SCHUBERT
Austria 1797-1828
Arr. by Henry W. Davis

Copyright MCMXXXVII by Rubank Inc.,Chicago,Ill.
International Copyright Secured

301-1

Barcarolle
from
Tales of Hoffmann

Jacques Offenbach although a German by birth, wrote most of his operas for the Opera Comique in Paris. Of his many successful works, The Tales of Hoffmann, from which this number is taken, is the most popular. The Barcarolle or Venetian Boat Song occurs in the third act. From a window in a Venetian Palace the canal can be seen in the moonlight, and two lovers are heard singing this beautiful melody while their boat moves slowly to its graceful rhythm.

Solo B♭ Clarinet

J. OFFENBACH
German-1819-1880
Arr. by Henry W. Davis

Copyright MCMXXXVII by Rubank Inc., Chicago, Ill.
International Copyright Secured

Largo

from

New World Symphony

Dvorak was a talented Bohemian composer, conductor and teacher.

At a very early age Dvorak showed remarkable talent for music. The New World Symphony was written by Dvorak when he visited America to direct the National Conservatory of Music in New York City. It is one of the most famous symphonies in the world.

B♭ Clarinet

ANTON DVOŘÁK
Bohemia = 1841-1904
Arr. by Henry W. Davis

Sleeping Beauty

Waltz Theme from the Ballet

Tschaikowsky was one of the first great modern Russian Composers to receive international recognition. He completed the Ballet Suite "Sleeping Beauty" in 1890 and considered it one of his best works. The "Thornrose Waltz" from which this excerpt is taken is the last number in the Suite.

Bb Clarinet

P. TSCHAIKOWSKY
Russian 1840-1893
Arr. by Henry W. Davis

Chansonette

Clarinet Solo

Bb Clarinet

A. M. BARRET
Arr. by A.W. Pazemis

887-1

Song of the Dawn

(Chanson d'Aurore)

from

Suite Miniature for Clarinet

Bb Clarinet

A. GRETCHANINOFF, Op. 145, No. 1

Edited by H. Voxman

902-1

Fanfare of the Poppies

(Fanfare de Coquelicots)

from

Suite Miniature for Clarinet

Bb Clarinet

A. GRETCHANINOFF, Op.145, No.5

Edited by H. Voxman

904-1

13

Homeward

(Vers la Maison)

from

Suite Miniature for Clarinet

Bb Clarinet

A. GRETCHANINOFF, Op. 145, No. 6
Edited by H. Voxman

906-1

14

Hunters' Chorus
from the Opera
"Der Freischütz"

CARL MARIA von WEBER
Austria 1786-1826
Arr. by Henry W. Davis

Solo Bb Clarinet

Copyright MCMXXXVII by Rubank Inc.,Chicago,Ill.
International Copyright Secured

308-1

Melody from
Concerto in Bb Minor

Bb Clarinet (Solo)

PETER I. TSCHAIKOWSKY
Arr. by Herman A. Hummel

917-4

Cantique de Noel
(O Holy Night)

Solo Bb Clarinet

ADOLPHE ADAM
Transcribed by G.E. Holmes

The Holy City

Solo Bb Clarinet

STEPHEN ADAMS
Arr. by E. DeLamater

2612-1-PL

Le Secret

INTERMEZZO

Bb CLARINET SOLO

LEONARD GAUTIER
Arr. by Henry W. Davis

Copyright MCMXXXVI by Rubank Inc., Chicago, Ill.   Copyright Renewed

B♭ Clarinet Solo

20
Frivolities
CONCERT POLKA

Bb Clarinet

N. K. BRAHMSTEDT

896-6

Carnival of Venice

Air Varie

B♭ Clarinet

HENRY W. DAVIS

940-4

Bb Clarinet

Clarinet Polka

Characteristic

Solo B♭ Clarinet I

TRADITIONAL
Arr. by Herman A. Hummel

Also published for Band arranged by Henry W. Davis.
Band arrangement may be used as accompaniment to this arrangement.

1013-3

Homeward
(Vers la Maison)
from
Suite Miniature for Clarinet

Piano

A. GRETCHANINOFF, Op. 145, No. 6
Edited by H. Voxman

907-2

Hunters' Chorus
from the Opera
"Der Freischütz"

Piano

CARL MARIA von WEBER
Austria 1786-1826
Arr. by Henry W. Davis

310-2

Melody from

Concerto in Bb Minor

Piano

PETER I. TSCHAIKOWSKY
Arr. by Herman A. Hummel

Cantique de Noel

(O Holy Night)

ADOLPHE ADAM
Transcribed by G.E. Holmes

Cantique De Noel

Cantique De Noel

The Holy City

STEPHEN ADAMS
Arr. by E. DeLamater

2613-4-PL

Le Secret

INTERMEZZO

PIANO ACC.

LEONARD GAUTIER
Arr. by Henry W. Davis

192-3

Frivolities

CONCERT POLKA

Piano

N. K. BRAHMSTEDT

Carnival of Venice

Air Varie

Piano

HENRY W. DAVIS

Elegante

941-4

Piano

Animato

Gran gusto

53
Piano

941-4

Clarinet Polka

Characteristic
Clarinet Solo, Duet or Trio

Piano

TRADITIONAL
Arr. by Herman A. Hummel

Also published for Band arranged by Henry W. Davis.
Band arrangement may be used as accompaniment to this arrangement.

1013-3